Down the Rabbit Hole

Kate Maxwell is a teacher and writer from Sydney. She has been published and awarded in many Australian and international literary magazines. Her first poetry collection, *Never Good at Maths* (IP Press), was published in 2021. Kate enjoys writing in many genres, including speculative fiction, flash and poetry. Her interests include film, wine and sleeping. She can be found at https://kateswritingplace.com/

Kate Maxwell

Down the Rabbit Hole

Acknowledgements

Poems have appeared or are forthcoming in *Cordite, Social Alternatives, Hecate, New Feathers Anthology, The Rush, Goat's Milk Magazine, The Poeming Pigeon, Camas, Last Leaves Anthology, Stick Figure Poetry, Brilliant Flash Fiction, Mocking Heart Review, Monday Night Magazine, Vita Poetica, River Paw Press, Gentian Journal, Backchannels Journal, Tether's End, Vita Brevis, Green Ink Poetry* and *The Alchemy Spoon, Other Terrain, Caustic Frolic, The Phare, The Timberline Review, The Wild Word, The Bangor Literary Journal, The Galway Review.*

'We Don't Live in a Tent' was commended in the
Goulburn Valley Writers' Competiton, *Tamba*, 2022.
'My Moon Man' was shortlisted in the
ACU Poetry Prize anthology, 2021.
'Let There be a Firmament' was shortlisted in the
Alice Sinclair Memorial Competition, 2022.

For Andrew and Max

Down the Rabbit Hole
ISBN 978 1 76109 507 8
Copyright © text Kate Maxwell 2023
Cover image: Rose Frasca

First published 2023 by
GINNINDERRA PRESS
PO Box 3461 Port Adelaide 5015
www.ginninderrapress.com.au

Contents

Part One: Before
  Fleeced ... 9
  A Mouthful of Carpet ... 11
  This Means Cake ... 13
  We Don't Live in a Tent ... 15
  Peak Hour ... 17
  Wasted on the Young ... 19
  In Your Mother's Garden ... 21
  Her Abundance ... 22
  Grounded ... 25
  Suburban Nativity ... 26
  Before You ... 28
  Meditations on Medici ... 30
  Incident in the Tunnel ... 31
  Waiting in the Car ... 32
  Queen of the Winter Flowers ... 34
  My Moon Man ... 35

Part Two: During
  Carroll Called it Fiction ... 39
  Gifthorse ... 41
  Terminal ... 43
  Water Pistol ... 44
  Heart Goes Out ... 46
  Hallowed be My Name ... 47
  We, the People ... 49
  True to his Word ... 53
  Loggerheads ... 55
  Swimming Lessons ... 56

Part Three: Continued

Let There be a Firmament	61
In Your Orbit	63
It Leaks	65
My Little Friends	66
You Never Said	68
How It Begins	70
Keys on the Kitchen Bench	72
I Can't be Bothered Writing This Poem	74
Fall of the Ratites	76
Hide and Seek	77
Pissant	79
The Grand Dame of Derision	81
The Deep	82
Broken Lines	84
The Kiss	85
Tick a Box	86
Sheltered	88
Phased	90
In Neutral-coloured Rooms	91
Compliance	93
Underwater Psalm	94
Pietà	97
Fallen Nomads	98
Your Connection was Interrupted	101
Skinny Words	103
Edible Weeds	105
Drift	108
Trickle Down	110
The Rest is Lies	112

Part One

Before

Fleeced

Such a city girl picking through the bush
like a soft-pawed house cat, shaking off
brambles spiky things, flying insects

and bush berries, some purple, bruised
blue, possibly good to eat – I wouldn't
know, won't risk it – that hang in fat fists

holding ancient secrets of survival tight
while sweat beads burst to sludge behind
my neck, the folds of my moist stomach

dampening shirt and desire to continue.
Day is sluggish. Still as suspicion. Haze
blurs the curves and crests of mountains,

the silhouettes of eucalypts, sets nostrils
twitching for that ever-dreaded whiff of
distant smoke. But thrashing through scrub

my foot lands upon a stinking sheep carcass
and then I smell nothing but decay. She's
flocked by buzz of adoring flies, her long

jaw slightly open as if about to comment
but thought better of it and simply laid aside
her woollen coat like an opera fur, exposing

pink, thin-membraned bowels. We hike back
to bridled homestead, crunchy gravel underfoot,
canopied by trellised vines, trussed-up roses –

crimson, blush, powder yellow, all bound in
wire-meshed frames, sustained by bore water,
like domed butterflies held captive in a desert.

Sipping chilled wine on floral dappled sofas
in air-conditioned rooms, we flicker through
Country Life magazines that show no gutted

beasts, parched earth and birthing maggots.
Instead, the glossy pages extol hills of rolling
green, stone walls, and fat white sheep from

foreign climes where city girls are given gum
boots for their country ramble and it's far too
cold for sheep to show their unfleeced underwear.

A Mouthful of Carpet

In my glimpses of the harbour
apartment, I groom my Pomeranian
        Mummy's puffy fur-angel
sip another chamomile tea
breathe in, breathe out
give in, give out
and pluck the lint of daily irritations
from my well-cut coat
        of respectability.
A dose or two of diazepam
sends me adrift, afloat
until I'm fluff and fibre-free.
News and world won't bother me.

Returned to glow
        lipstick set and blow
waved hair, legs crossed
at just the angle to admire
a slim ankle in Louboutin's
        I wait for callers
        or something
or settle for sleep.

From the balcony
way way down below
I see the shouting people shuffle
drop their suffixes
and dignities
climb over each other
like grubs, laugh too loudly
let themselves get fat
show their grimy bra straps.

So, I stay behind my screen
of gleaming glass
that the cleaner polished yesterday
and keep distance. Vivaldi
vodka, and mother's crystal
remind me how to rise
        when I have fallen
gagging on a mouthful
of wool-blend carpet
as I've snot wept
and clenched howls.

This Means Cake

2001

I suppose this means cake, said the principal
spreading texta-stained hands wide
to indicate much mighty celebration
much marked significance
in sugar, flour, eggs and butter
mixed to make us hungry for
that sweeter slice so often
promised in television tales
or patriotic recipes.

So, with blue shirts half-tucked
boys shoved and jostled in line
for a piece of green and yellow Australia
        licked icing from their fingernails
        throughout the long slow tick
of a pale and sticky history
afternoon.

*I only got a bit of Victoria. That's not fair
'cause Luca's got Western Australia
and that's much bigger,* they whined
and said Federation was boring
        I like McDonald's better.

Cake to celebrate the start and end
if not home cooked, a sponge sliced
into lamingtons or bought from American-
owned Australian icons that went bust.
      To be thrown at politicians
who've long forgotten Parkes'
idealism and were, as yet,
      not even *sorry.*

Still girt by sea but corseted in dry,
we keep trudging thirsty circles
into dust to catch our ocker tails.
While the Rainbow Serpent slithers
      under mines, around skyscrapers
      through colour-stripped coral,
      puckered mullock mounds
to survive: an ancient pulse.
Now the leaders proclaim,
      Let them eat cake!
My piece is sweet – a little dry,
      a little stale.

We Don't Live in a Tent

She said it often, and every time she did
I just imagined us all – sweating out our
summer nights under one big canvas shell

gauzed flaps for windows, crouched beneath
sagging roof and dim-lit lantern shadows
        fists of cards clenched into chests

        as we'd shit-grin shriek, *Go fish!*
All squeezed into folding camp chairs while
balancing foiled potato, coleslaw, charred

sausages on paper plates upon our sunburnt
knees then toppling sideways each time we
reached for the tomato sauce. A stinky bowl

of pilchards in the corner for the cat, who'd
probably then let one rip. So would Dad and
Johnno, as if enrolled in some vinyl-enclosed

contest to steal air. But I always liked the way
my tent imaginings made our little house feel
like a palace. *But even tents have doors, Mum*

I'd point out, *zippered and flimsy, but doors
nonetheless.* She'd just roll her eyes, tell me to
pull my head in and as I opened my mouth

to challenge that one too, she'd swat me with
the tea towel, throw a sliced carrot or, depending
on her mood, whack me firmly over the head.

Little shit, her weary eyes would say. But often
they twinkled too, half-proud of my smartarse
wrangling. I'd pay big to hear those words again.

But that door's closed now, like all those imaginary
tent doors. She'd get a giggle, though, knowing she's
my first connection each time I see an unclosed door.

That'll learn you, she might cackle from the clouds.
See what happens when you sass your poor old mum
 an eternity of nagging to shut the bloody door!

    But I will gladly take that precious perdition
as I search every day for unclosed doors and openings
just to spark a memory of her voice.

Peak Hour

It's that wet concrete smell
that lingers, pooled into corners
        a cigarette butt or two
maybe a soggy tissue, crust
of mouldy pizza that settles
just below your nostrils.
You want to itch, brush it off
but haven't a free hand
        clutching your plastic
        bag of going-cold curry
and ticket in the other. Stink
and grime and metal handrail
all ready to transmit the stink
and grime of everybody else
and everybody else
        is everywhere
        brushing against your side
your nerves, coughing, talking
loudly on their phones, filling
up the spaces with stale sweat
business shirts, hair-sprayed
heads and rounded bellies.

Even on a cold day, air is rank
and humid in the bowels
of the subway: sharp
tingle of iron, lapping up
body oils, farting back
metallic fumes
into over-peopled air.
So, you suspect the curry
may not last, could become
a gastric gamble if you miss
this next train. The platform
now so crowded and people
edging closer to the edge
of the yellow line with all
their curries, grief, and egg
salads, just trying to get home.

And no one is beautiful in this train.
Shoulder to shoulder, pore to pore
even the young and soft
so toned and tanned
but close up with congealed
globs of mascara

        in the corners of their eyes
or acne rashes rubbing cotton
collars. You close your eyes
dream of solitude and soap

        countdown to destination
for some hours of relief before
you do it all again tomorrow.

Wasted on the Young

I drive down Nicholson Parade
towards my mother's apartment
and I am seventeen and stupid again.

Spasms of my sublime insecurities
        flashes of the puerile past
shoot into my sensibly styled head

as I turn into her street. There I am
wheeling my Malvern Star and fragile
ego to the road, pulling down my fawn

checked uniform with one hand, steering
with the other, milk bottle legs glowing
in the sun, and mousey, all-lengths hair

flicking eyes and cheeks. Still wearing
that itchy woollen jumper in the heat
in case underarm stains show.

There's Sarah too, ingrained with gravel
and embarrassment, fallen from the back
of my bike: arse up, her knee and dignity

bruised, blushing to my betrayal giggles
as I fluster at the rowdy hoots and howls
of Year Twelve boys across the street.

And there's the bus stop where we'd wait
on days too wet or fresh to cycle. Where
Sarah's brother fitted on the grass one cold

morning, bus idling, driver out and standing
watch, the engine's growl chugging through
stunned silence as we watched, bug-eyed

while Sarah bolted home to fetch her mother
And clustered behind the pavilion on dark
sea-whipped evenings, we'd herd with sweet

Spumante bottles, stench of briny sewage
cigarettes, and seaweed tickling
at nostrils as we all pranced and postured

squatting on damp cement, lurching into limits
and each other with a foolish wet-tongued
fervour to be older. I'm fatter now

unable to hurdle the esplanade railing
or believe I'll *be someone,* yet I don't miss
that country of self-conscious cringe

bad hair and constant yearning. So, I park
the car, settle with pretending I was once
wild and free, and take my tea with mother.

In Your Mother's Garden

In your mother's garden, trees
– I can never remember their names –
stretch limbs above the old paling fence.

She has walked beneath pretty leaves
to point out flowering shrubs
perennials, rude weeds, but the names

fluttered away, escaping into pungent air.
        Beyond the cracked slate pavers
of a well-pruned courtyard, busy with bees

that hover over lavender and rosemary
and worker ants on jittery march across
rough-edged stones, we stretch

on soft grass. The big elm shades us
this afternoon. I flick a lost and itchy ant
from my ankle and turn the page.

You lie, quietly snoring, like a well-fed dog
while your mother hangs out washing –
        peach sheets and pillow slips

still water-heavy in warm air. *Claret ash.*
I remember now. A name to melt on
my tongue on this languid summer's day.

Her Abundance

We found a yellow-paged
'Famous Five' edition
behind the boxes of missing
pieces puzzles, some old
DVDs and chewed Lego blocks.

Then, in comic plum-mouthed
tones, she grinned into the dusty
weekend rental's gift
        leaned into the lounge
and her little performance

to recite a few excerpts of Enid's
loathing for the great unwashed.
Flicked out an earnest arm
        to scoff with glass
and eyebrow raised –

Oh, those filthy ragamuffins
who dare to bathe at
our respectable beaches.
Now they've simply gone
and spoiled the jolly picnic!

We cackled at her show
her abundant tolerance
        of intolerance, and yet
compelled by half-empty glass
I went and wrecked it all again

cast my shade upon the evening
spluttering on about so many
ordinary injustices, spurious blames
and blushing stupid in the bright
glow of her benevolence.

A generosity, hard to fathom
when her own ragamuffin:
        wordless, wild, resplendent
        in his own too big, too loud
world, so often raises eyebrows

of disdain, a chorus of complaint
that he too, be shunned from
bathing at respectable beaches.
        But she, with generous mouth
stretched to a thousand smiles

calmly insists that sunshine
is for sharing
        waters deemed too deep
        pathways thought too winding
must be coursed in kinder strokes.

And, on our Sunday morning walk
        before we packed the cars
        returning to our workday
        week, I cursed greying
skies, grumbled through

bare trees, fresh biting wind
but she bent low, stretched high
      to point out the wonder
      of new blossoms
while I saw only weeds and cold.

Grounded

Under dripping tap
he washes his pointy head
      sleek coal feathers
greased and gleaming
in the hot afternoon sun.

Crow hops crookedly
across the park, a creaky
old man, too long on horse
      bum high, awkward
as his slimy feathers leak.

Hurling cranky squawks
at round-eyed pigeons pecking
in the dirt, *Caw! Caw!*
he cries, half-raised wings
craning neck, a fisted threat.

Fat bobbing birds scatter
from his Darth Vader cloak:
      let him rule until dog
-time when sudden flight
fills the sky, the black sheen

of his elliptical extravagance
spread broad across
      a cobalt canvas
      and the grounded
      become glorious again.

Suburban Nativity

Day stretches like the loose smiled yawn
of Grandma's panting pug scratching
haunches up against the lounge. I check

the clock for this day – half yearned, half
dreaded – to be done while we, such paper-
hatted kings and queens, clink glass against

sibling stare, remembering only shattered
secrets, stolen toys, cruel pranks. In this baked
dinner dance of little snipes and grand gloats,

we slippery slide into the squabbling pouts
and jealous clutch of childhood. Mum will
drain the dishes. *I'll just rinse them*, she says

as I promise to heave myself from lounge
and help to steam and scrape the gravy-sticky
plates and platters. But I wake with Mary's heart-

glassed bubble bath pierced into my side
and find the washing-up miraculously finished.
Later, we watch shiny Santa hat celebrities

commanding grins from cancer-eaten children,
and somewhere, stuffed between the crackers
and the candles, Jesus – not sworn from a stubbed

toe – is named and pictured in my niece's mind
as yellow-crowned hero of the world
      Happy Birthday, Jesus, she whispers

to the rose-lipped idol on her card as she lines
her presents up beneath the tree in order
of determined worth: pink, pony and plastic

at the front, all clothes, and books behind.
And I ache to feel her calm, uncluttered creed
if only for today.

Before You

Loved before he knew the sky
tang of citrus, smell of summer
he gasped into the sharp air
of that late December morning
shocked by gravity –

        its heavy drag of cold
        and how his helpless
        unswimming limbs

flailed, so strangely unfamiliar
in this weird and wombless
world of too much light
and noise and touch.

Sobs hushed with the comfort
of sweet nipple, warm press
of skin on skin, and scent
and sound he'd always known
of her. She'd always known him
too. Had scrubbed and oiled
her strong-latched box of yearning

        long before he came
        each wish secured
        and wrapped with

tattered layers of a soul, stripped
and woven round his future.

Separate from affection
for the father: whatever she still kept
for that man, who turned away
gave so little until he gave
        the greatest gift.
Cocooned by freshly painted walls
blue as morning sky
        so unlike her daily
        shade of stoic sorrow
and clean white shelves lined
with folded cottons, bears or balms
to soothe imagined infant troubles

she rocked and crooned
        adored and swooned.
He had always been her life's work.
Magnificent as she moved
through this chosen devotion
        to channel, breathe and build
        a gifted passion for his joy.

Meditations on Medici

I don't gaze at ceilings and think of him
I don't think of him at all. His name
mentioned somewhere –
        in books or busts of blank-eyed heads
        droned by museum guides
        extrapolating on eggshell-blue
        conceit of clouds, names of naked torsos –
all in vague connection to the master
        of monument and masterpiece.
        A name: musical and Mediterranean
        but stirring no recall
                no renaissance
                or reverence.

Yet when I hear that other name
        the one all recognised
        rolling off the tongue
        like a many-syllabled song
I see, instead, a muscled arm
furrowed brow and marbled eye
squinting to the scaffold
with brush and dream and chisel
below his languid stretched forever
which millions have imprinted
as their ideal of heaven

        but the man who fed and made him
        that name –
        faded far into centuries
        like a forgotten ancient fresco.

Incident in the Tunnel

yells the flashing neon font above my head, all caps
and all inevitable, and goading me to skull slam into head-
rest, gasp a final breath of relatively fresh air before
the creep and clog of carbon monoxide fingers at the
flesh of my mouth, siphoning its ghoulish kiss deep
into lungs with thick grey fog of first world loss.
Tagged an incident, as if nothing ever happens in the
tunnel. Should we be happy for the tunnel? That this
vacuum of variety that only serves to get us here to
there is finally experiencing an event? Cocooned in
 concrete walls, blur of boring bitumen, those red flash
rectangles, before and behind, wail *stop, stop,* and *stop*
again. I cannot even *see* the incident: crane neck,
press cheek to window and see nothing but blocks of
farting metal impregnated with blank faces. A crack,
a stain – not seen at speed – draws my eye into its dark
and seeping rivulets of subterranean gloom, dripping
down suspended day into my middle earth fears of what
we're lodged below. Barely rolling rubber propels me,
inch by inch, and I'm still looking for the incident. A
death? A crash? A fit of road rage? Or was it just a burst
of balloons and honking horns to mark the millionth toll
customer crossing the invisible beeping line? Did they
thrust cake into the grasping hands of commuters quick
enough to wind windows down? Did balloons deflate,
hiss into drains, and wrap around some feckless fish far out
to sea? Eventual exit into daylight sets me blinking as I flow
into traffic's smoother pace and the incident's forgotten.

Waiting in the Car

while the men solve problems
inspecting damp courses
boot tips tapping concrete
and boldly undeterred
at staining moleskins with mud
        grass or machismo

they crouch, lie prostrate
to peer into sub floor cavities
        blocked drains, while
marking invisible distances
with flattened palms
or measured strides.

Shadowed in the humming
dusk of a low-lit street
I sink into passenger seat
        form chrysalis, spun
with memory's mitigating
silk, sheer shut-eyed fictions

all woven to entomb effort
solutions or necessary banal.
        My phone, and options
are flat in this steel chassis
world of coffee-stained
foam seats, stench

of cigarettes, crumpled
cheeseburger wrappers
at my feet, and metallic waft
of waiting   waiting
        waiting.
Then, when door's flung open

flooding car with light
and words like conduits
and causeways, I blink
        like a startled deer
stiff-necked, trying to recall
what that blinding light
of man means.

Queen of the Winter Flowers

She plants camellias under a chrome-coloured
sky to soften the short brick wall behind
      rearrange the pattern of her days
sweeten the air of a stale relationship
and colour the empty spaces
      on her envisaged canvas.

Diamond sparkles on her elegant right hand
      ungloved fingers flicking
      in and out of green
as we stand before stretch of shimmer blue
      but still, she reminds me sternly
      that it's not an engagement ring

and it's not what she wanted
      or even intended, but somehow more
      and somehow less.
A beauty, six foot of slender limbs
soft skin, yet nothing like
the pouting princesses of places to be seen.

Breeze slaps fresh, sometimes fierce
      as the vice of his cold benevolence
while we extol the moneyed ocean view
waiting for the men to finish espressos.
She sways through this beach house
      weekend like a dying swan.

My Moon Man

Some mornings, a grunt, a shuffle to the bathroom
where he'll soothe protracted post-child limbs
stretching out years, in steam and solitude.

His sinewed torso morphing into manhood
         a moon-mad beast simmering beneath
mottled skin, furrowed questions of his frontal lobe.

Other days, the flash of what was: a flicker
         of an unguarded smile, an accepted embrace
but mostly it's like picking paths through a spring lawn

full of bindy eyes; sharp glare of scorn, spiky words
pointed with armaments, prickling at every step.
I ease my tender-footed efforts to remain within reach

in sweet balm memories of silly songs, soft cheeks
         and gap-toothed grins, remembering
beneath heavy brow, red-rashed skin and tufty chin

there's still a child who loves his mother. One who
used to wrap himself into my warmth, cling to the
safety of my side, or prattle, big-eyed and loose-limbed

about dinosaurs and Lego castles. Who used to see
a soft-eyed queen, drew crayoned flower, yellow star
enchantments around our hand-holding shapes

         not this nagging frown-lined lady who's let
herself go. Let herself go to places you don't want to
follow: talkback radio, tax forms, mumblings of mortgage

empty milk containers, and the looping tedium of day
to day, so far removed from your imagined avatar
playing in your head: always rebellious, cool, remote

        the same one who cannot use a can opener.
And twisted in the knotted shoulders, casual cringe
you wear into the floodlight of the world's gaze;

        glaring hot, unshielded by childhood's comforts
is the realisation that you're now expected to perform
with no side prompter at the wings, no stage mum waving

actions from the floor. Unrehearsed, my mighty man
must leap and stumble, stand and bumble to an acidic
applause. A pitch still recognised in the cackle of that

unforgiving, *suck it up, Princess* sting, stabbed casually
by pack howls and snide splutters at every trip or slip
of exposed underbelly. I sigh into the sinew of your soul

so spare and raw now you've realised you're meant to
know it all and scared to show you don't. I would give you
shelter in my arms, my breath, save space for you

to crawl into my heart and hide, restore, or grow
        but you want none of it. No one must see
your soft insides, hear the simple succour of my consoling

words. We will pretend that you are grown and gone
untethered from that first finger grasp that never lost its hold
and deny our arms still ache to hold the other.

Part Two

During

Carroll Called it Fiction

Alice, Alice, just choose a door.
If you're waiting for it to be the right one
then you're obviously in the wrong dream.
Haven't you seen the news?
Doors can be alternative these days.
They all lead to somewhere
but even somewhere is up for debate.

All doors matter. Just open one
and if you grow too inflated for the house
then bust down the house, girl.
Want to join the Tea Party?
Grab a crock of conspiracy, take a place
where the noise never stops
the riddles don't make sense
but hey, it's a wild ride.

Or be a Dormouse. It's up to you.
Just stop whining about rules and traditions.
Education may have pushed you through those
portals but those doors are under renovation now.
You don't want to end up locked out, Alice.
The Queen, or King (nobody's really sure)
may look comical with painted face
such dainty hands and pompadour
        but they will still
        take your head.

Heed the Rose Garden warnings.
Watch those loyal soldiers
painting blue roses red, and remember
however farcical and futile they seem
those cards are stacked
much thicker than you think.

Follow the white rabbit, Alice.
It's easier just to fall.
Eat the cake. Drink from the bottle
labelled with little lies
and it'll make the world seem real.
And what is real anyway, Alice?
Real is what you believe.
Find that golden key
flashing in the comments thread
hidden in the web, in the chalice
of evangelical zeal.
Choose a door, Alice, and believe.

Gifthorse

This unexpected offer of hours, days
I would have once called possibility
and begged for its embrace
like a dazed teen groupie
ready to kneel and suckle on its glory.
Time's former crass dismissal
of my needs, no object
to this temporal adoration.

And once I'd named it master
Time stayed.
Splayed out its lazy limbs to lay
beside, caress the sinews
of its constancy. I stroked
and worshipped, ever grateful
for its crush of frantic rush
its henchmen wasting haste
with long deliberate breath.
And revelled in the way it tamed
that fast-twitch monster
who'd flung me task to task
from meal to sleep; now cowered
silenced, underneath the bed.

So, in the first flush of Time's love
it was my only captain.
But now, my lover bores me.
Stretching vowels, drawing out
each sentence and prodding me
to ponder, not the volumes waiting
on the shelf, nor the ever-changing
colours of the sky, the hum of a quiet
autumn day, but the chafing patches
on my elbows, an Internet quiz on
'Who I'd be If I was a Hollywood star'
and how to bake a loaf of bread
from tending stinking mould.

I could, do so many other things
with my blank boring lover
but sadly, Time and I
are not on speaking terms
and I will squander it, just for spite.

Terminal

Flight's cancelled. Clipped the wings of a skittish population
separated families, holidays to Bali, and global markets

with one swift shut down   lockdown   wind down
of our economic engines, no longer hoovering up air and fuel

or hapless birds that might easily send roaring sky monsters
and their many souls crashing into oceans of loss and curious

marine creatures. No more Flying Kangaroos outlined in blue
where neatly tucked stewards dish out nuts, napkins

and headphones to happy holidayers, bored businessmen
mothers dosing up toddlers on Phenergan. Now we drive past

rows of big metal birds, grounded on the still and silent tarmac
noses down, waiting behind fortified fences, broken budgets

for laid-off workers to hopefully return, and guide the raptors back
to skies where they are no longer lumbering beasts of dysfunction

but engineering marvels of the heavens delivering us to terminals
        where one day we may rise again.

Water Pistol

What you need is a water pistol: not pumped
with oxygen and hydrogen, but one-part bullshit
blocker, two-parts patience, holstered and ready
to squirt at rabid red-faced howlers who splutter
their cognitive dissonance in your face, at hardware
stores, on media mogul 'news', or the politician's
pulpit. All filling up our screens and minds with
blah blah blah until all that's left is that bloody
boring second amendment from some other stupid
country, so, you may as well bear arms for ears
and use that squirty silencer to shut the nutters up.

Of course, it may short circuit your device, enrage
your red-capped neighbour who seems confused
about which country they want to make great again
but the psychological relief of hosing down that
constant mouth crap releases like a deep cleanse
for the colon. Just ensure you shoot sharp and clean
into their always open mouths, for aiming straight
into the eye can make the blind see red, and then
you'll stand accused of communism or sympathies
to Canadian authors who paint all women red
in dark dystopian tales, no longer fiction.

Add some silver to the cocktail and it should work
on lobbyists and spinners too. A well-aimed shot
can leach out artificial toxins that trickle down
white collars in lying, brown stains. And while the
suits in charge applaud themselves for not shooting
shouting women on the parliament lawn, you might as
well weapon up. I'm not saying it can stop the babble
or re-attach loose parts, into what we once called
reason, but what you need is a water pistol. Go fill it
with your own concoction. Mine's two-parts alcohol
one-part hope but shoot up whatever works for you.

Heart Goes Out

But where does it go when it goes out?
Does it dress for the occasion; high heels

painted face, designer wear, stiff smile?
Does it wave polished fingers, flashing

white teeth and platitudes from a secure
location? Does it go out and read picture

books to children, sometimes dirty ones
in immigration camps, for perfect photo

ops? For hearts know not to judge people
by the colour of their skin, the contents of

their bank account, the God they worship.
Hearts know that a rose garden, lined with

crab apple trees needs supplanting. Best
to replace history with cold hard concrete

a perfect stage to don a mask, deadpan some
despair, and reiterate how hearts and prayers

go out all the time even when dressed in jackets
       that claim, *I really don't care, do you?*

Hallowed be My Name

It's been months since I saw my mother
Her lilting voice, repeated platitudes ooze
warm syrup in my ear: sweet, sticky tones

trickling down the line to clad the cracks
and channels of forgotten days. Her husky
laugh, my name held savoured in her mouth

the softest prayer. Such sacred love taken
for granted, like breath, the unbroken beating
of my heart, and sometimes I cannot even

make the call for fear that all her loneliness
will sliver beneath skin, burrowing deep
inside me for days. Easier to cover time

in dull endless tasks, deny the ache each time
I hear the cracking in her voice, the whistle
of an icy wind whipping at her solitude.

A carer brings her tea and biscuits to warm
the chill of her children's long absence.
I summon up her crinkled smile as she cries

'Oh, I've just been brought a lovely cup of tea,'
as if this will compensate for what we've done
to her, left her alone, now we're too busy

for the quaint hum of old love. And we will claim
this callous pandemic as the palisade that keeps
us apart but I know. I know your golden child

would rather bleed into the inky indulgence of all
those carefully placed words than have to suffer
the clear, searching gaze of her beloved hazel eyes.

We, the People

i.

Goody, Goody Two-Shoes
in 17th century Massachusetts
danced with the devil
on a cold cruel morning
spilt a bucket of warm milk
        upon cobblestone

was rumoured she'd done it
        on purpose, cared not
for cows, forgiveness
or the waste and spoke
no prayer. No prayer!
Just one of her impieties.

It's told her sins were bold
and many – sent a demon
plague to kill the crops
sicken the child and wield
the wicked winds.
        Did she repent?

Oh Lordy, Lordy no!
So, the whore's neck snapped
like white pine twig
when judgement came
and God and we, the People
        were satisfied.

ii.

Tempting still, to cap a roiling
rage in close-fitting coif
of flattened prim and plain
finger pointing, *click, click,
click* with coffee cup
        and cat's bum mouth

squeezing contempt like a well-
aimed feline sphincter:
        tail up and tapping
out domestic disdain
into fur licking
        frenzies of spite

        (Well, there's nothing
more definitive than a righteous
lynching to quash debate
on facts versus belief)
        but the thrills and spills
of roasting heretics, quoting

verse from ancient books
and white toothed testimonials
of head and shoulder
ringmasters who name
        the damned
will only take us back

to upturned bucket wailing
*I saw Sarah Good
with the devil! I saw god
and Rupert prophesise
that only true subscribers
will be saved!*

all pumped up in plastic
now, not fresh-faced
simple traitors of their sex
willing to be entertained
by watching Goody, Goody
Two-Shoes crack.

iii.

Round the screens and squeals
we go, shifting profiles
        allegiances to keep
        in flow. I have set
        my pilgrim's prayers
and apron to one side

watched you bleed, marvelled
at our matching shades
of red, even surfed the crowd
fund for your survival
        chance but when
        the crucible breaks

I lock arms with denial
greed and convenience
        plaster up the fissures
in my pride, rename my new
mantra worthy and wise
while we take the witches' eyes.

True to his Word

Not since the beginning of time
has there ever been, ever will be
        superlatives like this.

The greatest, most tremendous
of claims, each verse and gospel
to true believers

        intoned with untiring bluster
rust tan and chin-raised grandeur
steady, cocksure glare.

Whistled at the highest pitch
        that only true patriots
will hear, and dutifully heed

that flag-waving call, for the pious
and the proud to stand back
        and stand by.

For, never in the history of the
nation, was there a more facile
use of slogan

        more powerful promises
        accusations of things
we can't quite quantify

or clarify but know to be true.
For, never in the history
of this great democracy

have we known so much
with so little truth required
        for the superlatives

are sure and unquestioned.
Nobody does superlatives
like this, or ever will.

As it was in the beginning
        now, and ever shall be
            superlatives without end.

Loggerheads

When it came, the unfamiliar fear
to our comfortable first world lives
we thought it would come in bomb
shells, toxic fumes, exploding suns

but it crept inside us: lungs and hearts
travelled silent over skin and breath
resting in restaurants, subways, rooms
stealing air, and any reason to embrace

the other. Masked, as just another virus
it plucked wisdom from the fearful crowds
which some claimed, insignificant –
their time was done. Our harder hearts

exposed, squeezed by politicians' panic
and splutterers of spin. Brought fools
leaders, then countries to their knees
but not in prayer, humility, or gratitude.

There was no blockbuster moment, no
grave-toned president uniting nations
with steady gaze, old white man words
but the throat tightening realisation

that we are not nation, just disparate
tribes, beating chests, scared of each
other, scared of the sun, and scared
that our reckoning has finally come.

Swimming Lessons

When it starts
lapping at your toes
that creeping tide, at first so cold
you flap arms, become a gasp
      of breathy shock
dip in, dip out, like a water
wary cat trying to shake
an ocean from your hide

but pussy footing at the edges
just prolongs the chill
while you shiver with dilemma
to dive, turn back or drown.
Sliding slowly to its pull
as sand beneath your feet
sifts in, sifts out
you drive heels

into an ever sinking surface
crash and shock and thud
pounding always in your ears
and swell now pushing
at your knees:
hard to hold your ground
in all this spin
as it froths and bubbles

slams reason and resistance
until it's easier to just get swept away.
You're adjusting
to the temperature
in fact the air around
your unsplashed limbs
becomes a cold reality
        you'd rather refuse

so, you start to place faith
        in submerging
hum along to songs
of kindred souls beneath
who've broken surface
sirening their shared belief
that only weak
and fearful drown.

        You take a breath
and plunge. Shock of water's
tingling grasp
tickles along skin
and for a moment
freedom is exhilarating
        until you remember
        you never learned to swim.

Part Three

Continued

Let There be a Firmament

Firm footed over centuries, palms pressed to hips
or leaning heavily on hoe to take a thirsty swig
we took pause to peer at birds soaring into blue

tracked fading curve of wings into the brilliant
blur of eyesight's limits and wondered what
they already knew. Secrets of the birds stayed

hidden many years. Tower building, mountain
scaling to mimic avian views, we scanned seas
cities, plains, and saw only flat horizons falling

into hazy unexplained extinction. Knew nothing
beyond our selves, so gave ourselves forever –
claimed earth, a holy tabernacle between heaven

and hell, sun, and seasons merely whims of gods
and demons. So much easier to grasp such deified
benevolence or sanction, then the yet uncharted

truth; that earth just spins its furtive sliding roll
beneath our very feet. Myths and creeds made
fillers for our mind's black holes, empty spaces

shimmering with storied stars of hunters, lions
and bears, all pitched in silver fight or flight above
our tiny heads. In ancient India, when gazing into

night some declared our globe secured upon
the backs of monstrous elephants, which in turn
stood upon the back of a colossal turtle, forever

swimming a black and waterless ocean. And even
legend's boy, who flew on wings of feathers and
wax to search the vast unknown found no answers

in the inky void but fell to earth in melting shame
of imagination's limits. Icarus, first space traveller
who flew too close to the sun, another fiery caution

to our astronomical yearnings. Best to keep faith
in accepted lies and frail absurdities, burn detractors'
words and bodies at the stake, those who dare to pose

the brittle possibility, that we may not be the centre
or reason of all, but simply specks in a universe of
floating specks. Still, in our science-saturated world

with tested hypotheses, men upon the moon and planet-
sized brains continuing to unmask answers of the aerial
abyss, some still claim comfort in a dark age disregard

of awkward truths, preferring fiction and alternative facts.
I too, concede a reverenced terror of the air-sucking beyond
still chills my veins each time I stare too long into the night.

In Your Orbit

You, celestial body spinning
centrifugal, luminous
        and spreading silver
to the reach of my optical lobe
need no telescope to magnify
the truth: how you'll expand
my universe exponentially
        each smile a shimmer
        through time and space
        each touch a continuum
of quivering forevers.

These heliocentric days of your
radiance
        balm to all those frigid
        nights and colder seasons
where I'd spin, lost in shadows
        spiralling with dull desires
        gloom too dim
        and dissolute
        to find your face.

And science cannot explain
        how you were formed
exploding, star-shaped
in my soul with white hot
force, propelling yourself
ever outwards
to cluster in my cells
like oxygen.

Then, when you drift
how panic thins the air
until I'm gasping
tube-tied
tethered only
by the thought of you.

It Leaks

It Leaks.
Dripping tap.
I've asked you to shut it tight.
Plop, plop, it fattens and falls
splat, onto my nerves
as you glance, eyebrow
cocked, and Mona Lisa
smirking at my twitch.

I've asked you to shut it.
That dripping tap
with rhythmic irritation
seeps into my skull.
Plop, plop, plop
and I will not get up
to feel your amusement
        at my back.

My Little Friends

I send them with a click, a sigh
whisper, with a clench-toothed smile
You bloody words perform, or I will twist
and wring the guts out of every inky letter
then shut the laptop down
and walk away to brood.

Dead poets are dead, leave them be
I tell myself while labouring
on a reading, fawning over someone
else's words and trying to discern
why mine lie down to show their soft
bare tummies, *Here mock me! Kick me!*

Now, I just believe in publication
       if I have to buy it, lie it
or change my name and leanings
to something with more edge, I will
limp about without my punctuation crutch.
I'll do it.   Just not for this poem.

So, I sit and wait for words to return
often travelling with a few new ones
Thank you but we cannot place your work
We hope your piece finds a good home.
But I'm not running a bloody shelter
for homeless prose

so, I give the whimpering mongrels
one more chance, scrub them down
remind them how to beg
 before I send them out the door
again. Then I'm back to coffee
shops and writers' meetings, listening

to portentous speech, pretending
to relate, and grooming words
whatever colour and style is going down.
I write myself a Post-it note
then stick it to the wall:
I look forward to seeing more of my work.

You Never Said

Around the negative spaces
of your nose, ridge
       of your lips
I've marked regret.

Grain of your skin is coarse
with dour dismissal
of long, indentured days
       spent laying bricks

of someone else's agenda
       tabulating
       the tedium
of others' commands.

Strange, the way your irises
deflect that everyday
displeasure
crinkled into grey green

smiles and stoic sighs
       of day to day
but now, eyes wide shut
flickering conceded dreams.

Sealed in by my own
heavy curtains of grief
       back dated, grim
          blocking out the light

I'm shamed by stale expulsion
of such secret despair
       and roll away
from your sleeping lament.

How It Begins

You don't scare me
with your compliments
the way you stand so close
brush fingertips along forearms
hold my eye too long
        softly wind
        your winning smile
around tissues in my optical lobe
so shaken up with your motion, form
and shards of all your silver words.

        Knock me out. I dare you.

Pitbull persistent in scent
of all intruders
        those with careful
        knowing aim, affections
        learned, then quickly feigned
I've traced undertones of ethanol
in your sweet, layered scent
a hidden hunger in your keto breath
that sears a stale, hot kiss
over pale uncherished cheeks.

        Turn off the light. I dare you.

So, now you wait
in dirty shadows, just to
        watch, crawling into
        holes or fears unlocked
and all under the guise of good
all to gather what you could of
any use. Cat-pawed, you creep
into the emptiness I've long accrued
and sucked within my stoic
cold, seek shelter in my solid hold.

        Stay with me. I dare you.

Keys on the Kitchen Bench

Nothing in the letterbox or behind the second pot plant
on the porch, no scrawled note, or objects of unspoken
reminiscence, no

        packages of sorrow seeding damp disintegrations
to erasure – their salty spread of soluble mapping vast
and creeping lands

of pain across brown paper skin, separating soggy fibres
once tangled tight together, into ungrateful air. So, were
you even here?

Flashes of your face, your smile, or sneer beyond my chin
fingers trailed along my thighs, your twice worn T-shirt
crumpled, funky on the floor

        but nothing now. Nothing in the night beyond slow
switch of liquid crystal digits on the clock, hum of mocking
hours, half-empty

double bed, and ever-changing plans to start again tomorrow
fill my days with caffeine, forced matte smiles, and vague
unfinished tasks.

No more messages beyond those final words that whisper in my head at every boring presentation, lonely lunch, late television dinner.

No brief enquiry of my health, opinions of the latest, or the little moments left behind, the brackish aftertaste of memory's taint I filter

through quiet tears. Did you lose memory of my face? My shape my heart? No deliveries of final touch, let-down missives to ease. No conveyance at all.

I Can't be Bothered Writing This Poem

Dull gristle-coloured days where television
sways banal fantasies before our faces
and YouTube pouts and shimmies
>
> all with impossibly long legs
> tight skin, and all of it wrapped
> in the latest brands, latest catch
> phrase and all available
> to pause

so we can refill our glass, pop more pills
and pop-up treats, while seeping like warm
syrup, and flattening our saggy arses into
the catatonic hold of couch cushion shapes.

Fold upon fold, flesh rippled over flesh
we watch our sucked in selves squeeze into
beige shapewear before the bedroom mirror
>
> but thank the gods that we don't
> see each other's gurgling insides
> all that rancid lusting smallness
> of our soft and sad internals.

And on this gristle-coloured day I'll spit
a smile out for the bored cashier's
  Have a nice day, and by the way
I couldn't give a shit. Later, on the lounge
I'll prattle my media-fed philosophies
at you, at me, in front of the TV.
  But no one's listening.
  Not even me.
  So, I'll throw my fork
  dripping with gravy
  at the pink curve of your ear
while screen flickers and rumbles.
What did you say?
  Forget it.

Fall of the Ratites

How you are fallen from heaven, O Day Star, son of Dawn! – Isaiah 14:12–13

Lost my strong pectoral muscles generations past
soaring through mountain mists, heaven in my heart
breath of blue, now but a tingle in the flap and flutter
of these heavy useless wings and upward yearnings.

Of stones and dirt, not wind and clouds, these broad
fat feet will claw and search, eyes down and roosting
into gravity with stoic resignation, obligated surety
that we remain sustained, since earthbound and enlarged.

Weighed down with the heft of durability, thick bodied
tough skinned, and breastbone now too flat to use as keel
I pause in my pedestrian foraging, scan unending skies
to watch those of us still able-winged and hollow-boned

hover and sail as they touch edges of forever with their
feathered tips and lighter souls. Down here in the dirt
squinting into sun and splendour, their aerial abandon
still whispers to my armless torso, *once, you also soared.*

Hide and Seek

I've been trying to read words.
Words that play hide and seek
      with meaning.
Come and get me! they squeal
running off in run on sentences
grinning at the gist of ideas
luring with their pretty rhythms
set out, just so
with   spaces
in all the right places
a tilt, maybe an innuendo
a clever disorder to frame order
coquettish fragments
but never quite specific

just a dropped
      word

      a skipped line
to sharpen senses
into a tantalising tease
of something, clearly something
of significance but no one's game
to ask exact intention. Point's been
missed and poet will be surely pissed.

Luscious whispers, graceful phrases
posing on the tips of tongues
pushing lips to pout
such clever, shapely choices
that build to promises
of a revelation, a meaning to it all
but end up trailing into
        unfinished

Those open pulsing lines
left to the perception of Dear Reader
to feel and know and feel.
Slippery words that glide and slide
like midnight skaters
cutting cross the icy page.

I've been trying to read words.
This time I'll catch them
hold them down, while they avert
their pretty shapes, try to flutter off
but I will bore into their inky printed
symbols and rip their fucking faces off.

Pissant

This Saturday of shining grass
and yawning cat
shimmers about my hair
as I weigh down the paper
        old version, once wood pulp
with coffee cup and frown.

A ball of brown-beaned warmth
at the cusp of my neck
        is my sigh
my breath, a sieve
to filter melancholy.

Black ink presses into elbows
        thoughts. Words
capitalised or ugly bold
splutter forth of angry souls
with flags and flame
who stare into foreign lens
hear only explosions
breathe only dust.

I deny the world its news
flip over to the lifestyle section
new restaurants, ways to dress
and think, yet pulse still hums
along that headline shot
of crumpled bodies in logo T-shirts
loose-limbed as contortionists
surrounded by rubble.

There's a tree in the photo
gangly as a teenager
in the middle of the street
surviving the explosion
with a rooted grim resistance
that the dead boys
        thought was theirs.

Now, a plum-bottomed ant
scuttles up the wooden table leg
flickering on paper's edge
        I blow it off, not bothering
        to watch it fall
as I shake the pages clean
and return to my shining
grass-scented Saturday.

The Grand Dame of Derision

With yellow eyes, unsmiling stillness she stares
So contemptuous of my unfeathered, inedible form
that keeps her fed and warm but closely caged
from flickering, twittering scurrying pleasures.

Yawning fish breath in luxurious boredom
she is elegantly efficient with disdain; prefers
to serve it cold from the windowsill, scratching
claws on the back of the couch, or flicked from

a pale pink tongue licking fishy remains stuck
round her paws and whiskers patterned bowl.
Sultry eyed and swathed in fur, the grand dame
of derision saunters over to pause   preen

in front of the computer screen. Annoyed, I push
her off the desk only to be shot with upturned tail
and hiss, so she sits, paints her shining coat in spit
and fashions an acid yellow stare of feline scorn.

The Deep

She stood by riverbank
        a fool in love with life

        while silence bounced about
        her ears and smiles itched
at her lonely lips.

Beneath the bridge
        dumped trash and used
        affections
melded into mud, rust-embalmed
received brown
        lapping river love.

Sliding feet from sticky shoes
she waded into wet embrace
        sweet shake and shiver
        pressing to
        forgotten thighs

while water washed and rocked
and crooned
>> *not too cold, now*
>> >> *not too cold*
ran ripples through her reedy
>> hair, beguiled and whispered
>> *deeper, deeper*
>> >> *do you dare?*

Releasing to the river's heart
>> her pulse a sinking
>> thrum
>> of fading dreams
but held so close and held
so deep
>> she sent out sighs
>> and flowed into forever.

Broken Lines

All those Kamikaze poets nose diving into too much nothing
picturing plummet's thrill, but ending
with an earthly thud, a crash, a curious cow
snorting at broken lines, dismembered words
all splattered cross a depth of field that poets
        non-numerical, could never guess.

All those preposterous poets disembowelling
emotions onto white snickering pages
now, sadly oven-gassed or sinking
in the puddles of their leaking sanity
should have spent more time reorganising
sock drawers or scrubbing bathtub rings.

When I've caught myself dressing in red underwear
to pen a poem on bushfires, or leaping from
        the shower, wild-eyed as a hound in hunt
          just to snatch some words in water bleeding
ink I picture the rolled back whites of those
dead poets' eyes and embrace my mediocrity.

Even in red underwear, my muse has short attention span
hankering after Netflix and internet pandas.
On odd occasions when I've crammed too much into my brain
for it to turn its teeth on me: spitting out tortured
        text inventing new epiphanies, I've vowed only
to play Candy Crush and watch the shopping channel.

The Kiss

Why do they eat so much lipstick?
Apparently, in a lifetime
more than their own weight
consumed in every
        traffic light stop
        toilet break
        and corridor waiting.

Often flaked
like drought-dried mud
or just a faint 'O' shape
fading into outline.

When I leaned to kiss her
at the door, she tasted
like musk detergent
and left me with
a pink tooth-stained smile
and urgency for tissues.

Tick a Box

These words, drawn from dreams
plucked from what my eyes see
my ears hear, what my body
      feels, are merely mine.

Not his, not hers
      not black, not blue, not binary
and neither are they related to
the regions of my crotch
and who or what I choose
to rub it up against.

These words come with no
disclaimer, no caveat of how
this writer worships
which race or creed
the writer identifies as theirs.
Words identify themselves
      so often scrawled
      in the vernacular
      of country, class, beliefs
and tip towards a box
before I can break them up
or scold them into scattering
away from comfortable
four-cornered lures.

Standard, loose or lovely
Avant Garde or classic
        they spread over a page
to prove a point, paint a picture
play against or with intention

        and sometimes
they place themselves upon a page
like they have here, and refuse
to tick a box
even though my name
and head shot do.

Sheltered

Kittens froze last night.
Underneath the open porch steps
where wind and sleet wailed banshee
song all night, I found them
>crinkled to the dry teats
>of a stupid skinny she
who couldn't find a shed, a sewer
a warmer place to birth

their never opened eyes just frosted
slashes, mouths tight as stitches.
Prodded with my thick-soled boot
I unclasped one from the stiff pelt
of its mother. This little temporary
taxidermy fraud
>that I could mount upon the
mantle until it dripped and thawed
reached rigor mortis arms to me
>but I blew vapour clouds
into the bitching air, turned my back
and left it for the garbage man.

Hearts cracked last night.
Unsought, the cashier offered
with my coffee, news;
>	how the old man along her hall
>	just, *up and froze to death.*

And all the upwards journey
in elevator's thicket of husky
>	coats and smells

into the stuffy warmth of office
I imagined that old man
ribs cracking with his final breath
and frigid as those frozen kittens.

I woke late last night.
Your cold feet, like swords
slashed against my legs and I burrowed
beneath feathered quilt to spoon
into your sleep.   Maybe
the same moment as the kittens' last
or the old man's sad surrender
>	to the sift and shred of winter.

Phased

>Shouldn't be there at all
>behind the roof tiles and
>stretching skyward branches

breaking blue like an audience
gasp, mistake, forgotten sock
or mumbled apology.

This thin communion wafer
pocketed for later
>its sacred covenant

suspended, awkward in the
light of ordinary anomaly
>and sunlit outrage.

Slice of unblacked orb
hung over in the bright
>mocking glare of morning

now pale, grey, and waxing weary
>stayed up way too long
>stayed way too high

overshot, now squinting
through unallocated space
and caught out in its underwear.

In Neutral-coloured Rooms

Think of something peaceful,
          she said. Maybe she meant
something that won't send my Fitbit
flashing, blaze my cheeks, constrict
my larynx with a way too fast inhale
of fuck-it-all exasperation fermented
from the almost daily sharps and smirks
cacophony of commentary infesting ears
and eyes each time I pass a billboard,
click a post that thrusts its flesh, fat
or faith into my face in endless
liquid crystal display.

Think of something peaceful,
          she said, offering me the same
expression I've seen so many times on
so many screens: an avatar of concern
and dark blazer-wearing professionalism
boring deep into my skull with dollars
and degrees. But all I found was a
memory: a photo seen somewhere
of long-haired youths with daisies
shoved behind their ears, saluting
peace as they puffed their paisley
serenity into blue.

Okay, I'm thinking,
        I said, as she waited, the line
of her mouth stiffening with the effort
of feigned patience. Still, I could not
get past those unwashed hippies
in their psychedelic T-shirts, so
I pretended to keep searching
for solace in my soul.

I'm thinking of an empty foreshore,
        I lied, built a sigh,
a crumpled brow to show
I knew the worth
of visualisation
        yet still musing
on the slow-drip honey hum
of an opiate-assisted daisy dream.

Compliance

If the wind had fingers, it would prise open
the classroom window, stretch its bony digits
down the blackboard in a scraping, banshee wail.

It would howl through corridors and lessons
upending, and unnerving all. We'd clasp hands
over our ears, hair stiff on our forearms, and

shudder out the wind's whining song into walls.
Imagine Miss Jones' poppy eyes bulging as papers
and panic flew about the room. Lucky then, that

wind remains formless: fussing loudly in the leaves
flapping the shade cloth back and forth, but unable
to grasp it in a fist. Still, it demands our attention

shaking and clattering the windowpanes, knocking
over trash cans. We twitch and gasp, admiring its
outbursts like the way we relish Harry's bad behaviour:

fun to watch the carnage from the safety of our seats.
But now we're told to sit. Stay calm and focus on our
tests. 'It's just the wind,' Miss Jones snaps, then gives

Harry her special warning stare. And, as if enraged at
such vague dismissal of its power, wind howls its
fingerless rage at us. Hissing and huffing, rattling the

glass, and teacher's nerves. Neck bent, we scribble
words and words while wind blows and blows. Even
Harry is quiet. Wild is the wind but tame are our hearts.

Underwater Psalm

Below, but not too far from breath
        and sky, cloistered
in the briny nave of ocean's vast cathedral
warm-blooded beasts sleep
        in arcs of vertical silence.

Colossal monuments,
mysterious as Salisbury's standing stones
        – their huge heavy heads
still, beneath lapping line of dome
and sea where god's sigh

over waters deemed dominion
yet served no shield from arrogance
above.   They sleep,
        perchance to dream
one eye open, one, half conscious

to continued breath, too close teeth,
vessel's leak of earth's black
spills or sudden shot of spear
        and sway
below swells of shifting surface,

unbroken for now as their semi slumber,
        legion of deistic dreamers
or smoothness of the ocean floor.
Sad songs quiver through the deep
to moan the sacking

       of their holy places
from those who rock and reel above
       in big and little boats,
drill holes in subterranean seas,
cetacean's spines, throw death

and plastic into coral gardens,
make chase with harpoons and binoculars
       cast nets and nets and nets
       until sometimes
these huge prophets sigh their last

pondering if death, too, delivers
mournful dreams.   We watch
slow tide formations line the weeping
shore with a waste to rival
       our best destructions.

But today, not too far from breath
       and sky, in walls of water,
       thick with tiny life
and swimming things that glide
or drift in glorious hush

slicing aqua shadows or billowing
through dancing seaweed,
       these blubber-built pillars
pointed to forever in immaculate
suspension, sleep

where only muted psalms of sea,
        the pulse and pound
        of sonic prayer
suffuse this liquid sanctuary.
        A faith I'd surely follow,

if only I could fill my lungs
with more than blight and bitterness,
immerse my breath
        and sink my heart
into these songs of deep belief.

Pietà

His head rests on my shoulder now.
As a child he'd nestle there.
When the shadows grew, my boy
tired from loves and labours of the day
would rest as I stroked his hair.
We'd walk along the riverbank
gathering rushes.
In the still, waiting dusk
poppies blazed and the chill
of changing seasons made me shiver
as I pictured years to come.

His head rests on my shoulder
cold-cheeked and grey.
At the close of this long dark day
he lies bloodless, wasted in my arms
as I stroke his matted hair.
Stretched on groaning timber
his arms spanned
a world of sorrow and fear.
Forgotten hero to the riot
of soul-scared people at his feet.
My son. God's Son.

Fallen Nomads

A bag of coal
earned scavenging at the tip
– toxic too, but now the last alternative
to frigid slow starvation on the steppe
will stop his children freezing in the yurt
while blanketing all in benzene
fug of carbon monoxide; its sulphur-
smelling warmth seeping lungs
and brains, only to postpone end
       to different days,
          more gradual design.

Not so long ago,
he rode; a grassland lord,
resplendent in brightly coloured deel
while herding goats, horses,
       the weight of tradition
– just like his ancestors,
trotted out in sepia-toned archives,
all mounting and dismounting
at staccato speed, flicking braids
and pride, wide smiles aimed
at camera lens and sunshine
with no trace of tomorrow's
dissolution.

Now, clinging to the littered outskirts
of the world's most polluted capital
this nomad sells scrap
to recycling companies
in a satirical cheap segue of survival.
        The rush and sting of snow
        upon cheeks while cantering
        the wind, delicious bite of fresh
        and fierce, dissolve into blur
of Ulaanbaatar's smog
as he rummages in dirt
for coal and coin.

Bitter silence of that morning
still storms his restless dreams
– such unnatural hush,
        not a bellow or bleat
just the raw squall of air
trapped deep inside his thumping heart
when he saw so many frozen
carcasses, hard hooves in the air,
some half buried, some still
whimpering of dzud's white death
at minus forty degrees.

All his life
spent riding, walking
        by their round furred sides,
        soft muzzles tickling his palm,
        familiar scent of grassy breath
        and woollen warmth,
all lost in nature's final slamming fist
upon earth, furious at our relentless toll.

Your Connection was Interrupted

by thick timber walls of intolerance
concrete hearts, unpaid bills

but mostly severed by a sucking
swallet of will and water pooled

within our skin, brains and bones
flooding us with fear and bigotry

        short-circuiting ourselves
so we won't flow into the other.

You could tread water for days
dog-paddling a sea of screens

until water-heavy limbs collide.
The touch of 'other' then seems all

        too slippery, too suspicious
in these tepid shallow streams

where floaters drift: their troll turds
threatening to stink you up with virus

spread and stain. Daily clicks and down-
loads provide a plethora of ways

to drown, weighing down with all caps
one-sided commentary that calls itself

debate yet splattered with expletives
locked-door bravado, hate

compelling us to cancel or condemn
in ever-changing currents of disdain

      while mercenaries wield silver
spoons to stir up swells of spin and spite

      reminding our soporific selves
that it's not big business, bricks or oceans

blocking me from you but it's our neighbours
we must blame for interrupting our connection.

Skinny Words

I'm leaving these words
        on the page
sliced but undressed
without their garnish
of alliteration
tang of saucy subtext.

I will serve them fresh
        cold
        and call them
deconstructed poem.

Usually prepared
with tempered
precision
        here they sit
        callow, pale
and blandly waiting
for the tip of my pen
to stir or toss them about.
Not today.

No basting with a second
guess or searching
for the perfect
way to plate.
These words are raw.

Read them.
They won't make
you fat. They won't
make
        anything
at
                all.

Edible Weeds

I pink flesh bawled into days
the year a tardy referendum
condescended to bestow
original owners
        a place
        in the population –
as if this were the year of arrival
as if we'd never noticed
ever-glowing embers
hypnotic drone of hollowed wood
bodies melding into trees, country
towns like heat-hazed landscape
        seen only in sun-blinded
blur, grim shadows of tradition
convenient lack of clarity.

        Still two more years until
that giant slow-motion leap for mankind
streamed into our lounge rooms
        bubble-headed heroes
kicking space dust, colonising
satellites to thrill our still wanting-more
eyes: not mine, more likely fixed
on wooden pull-along dog
and sippy cup of orange crush
        while flags were pitched
over countries, moons and babies'
wrists, all waving cotton, iron or plastic
bracelets of possession
        tagged and taken minutes

>   from first breath
>   a dreamtime away
>   or an airless black
>   of distance ruptured.

Yet another year of moments
that changed history
>   but only flickered on a screen
>   or inked a page as snags
>   and mashed potato went cold
– our daily dose of blight or brilliance
before bedtime.
>   Same old shocks of new and never
>   before, mind in dimmed appal
>   I've seen it all before.
You'd have to Jesus shuffle over water
fill my soul with exclamation marks
shed skin and glow like hot rocks
to restore my shock and awe.

Now, on this day, I want nothing
>   maybe a garden of sunshine
>   slow pulse, warm dog
>   but mostly still, and mostly
>   nothing.

But, always somewhere in the cracks
of all this dirt and stone grow
        dandelions: bursting yellow
        salutations till withered bones
        are blown to breeze
        floating benevolence
like fairy dust into my weary lungs
to build another candle-blowing breath.

Drift

Stretched your tubular tendrils out
from square of earth, you call home
        it's nutrient lode of love
        shading boughs, entwining
        clutch of too close ivy
and become airborne.

Thrill of cool air, glow of variegated
leaves, before unseen
        now floating in your undetermined
drift. Soft fall into foreign soil
        that for a while, feels supple
grazing at your sides, such different grain

        and oh, the fecund thrum of colours
clustered swaying sun-worshippers
so reed thin and elegant
        all pulsing in the heady scent
        and thud of chlorophyll
        coursing through your core.

And yes, you shed a little
        parch in too bright sun
        don't drink enough water
but briny breeze, new field of friends
and a springtime of freedom
        means you hardly feel your feet.

You're not evergreen, after all.
        Surely, meant to seed and stretch
        beyond immovable old roots.
Slowly, though, you start to understand
        the end: this wane's not
        mere fallow sleep of winter

no new seasons here but scorch and shine
sucking air from lungs of earth
        so, you shoot out desperate fingers
into dirt which faster friends already fled
        and see your haven: loamy, loose
        and shallow

blossoms blown to cultivate the new.
Wilted, wistful for the rich embrace
        of home, you cling, frantic
with the ragged scrub of other
weedy regrets and wait while
        hoping for a strong wind.

Trickle Down

Single playground tap, ever dripping into dirty
brown puddle – plink, plinks its metronome of shame

that council won't fairy godmother it into a shiny
water fountain, maybe throw in a new amenities block,

some play equipment too. But no. No money doled
out for those whose vote won't count. *Look what they*

did to the bloody skate ramp, says the ash-flicking lady on
morning smoko, puckering little lines about her lips

and heart, *all tagged and trashed from those stoners*
puffing bongs down in the storm drains! Field of buffalo

grass, rusty swing, one tap, and leaking toilet stalls
that sober parents ban their kids from using, but just

enough to kick a ball, stretch subway or apartment legs
into a sprint. *All good, all good, see?* so the council man

says, sucking up a Sprite and small corruptions at his desk
while his 'Yes' team nod like bobble-headed dogs upon

a dashboard. *All good my arse!* mutters the tired woman
minding her neighbour's kids and own as they throw sticks

and spit into each other's howls, tire at taking turns
on the one-chair squeaky swing. Still, better than custard

and chips getting shoved into the lounge cracks that won't
be found until her mother visits, when she delivers

Ajax and disappointment to her door. So, she wipes up snot
and sorrow, brings back half-smiles with soggy french fries

before buzzing her neighbour's apartment – as long as he's
not there. As long as he's oozed into someone else's problem,

fading out like their mother's purple bruises. And that bloody
playground tap, plink, plinking in the still of night, soaking

up wasted water into one single square of earth: tap-tapping
in the temple of the semi-conscious junkie, sprawled out

on concrete toilet floor, who dreams of swings and sunny days
beyond this one-tap park. *Higher, higher!* he hoarsely pleads,

while retro painting memories from monochrome realities
he'd rather just forget, and tapping out, tapping out.

The Rest is Lies

It's not home –
        concrete, walls, a boarding pass
throng of strangers, unmade bed
same seen for months, same bricks
and AC unit outside the window you can't open.
Some sleeping man, scent of sweated
cotton, words scattered through a day
        and recognised, some not
        some sounding like song
twang, a throaty code of secrets
plots to overthrow your dinner plate
or mock your gweilo ignorance.
        But eyes still offering the same
bored, mildly curious or bland
reminding you it's not home, not country
not yours, maybe not theirs either
        just space and ground
        and bubbled allocations.
Here's your part. Here's mine.

Then you take things out of bags and boxes
place them into slots and shelves
inside the square you've claimed
with coins and papers. Daily toil
to hoist the flag of unreal estate
we all call real which mostly
        feels ridiculous.

While mother festers
        boxed within her walls of keeping
where they keep her warm and fed
keep her in and keep her out
of rooms with chipped crockery
private dreams, hip-breaking stairs
and peeling wallpaper
        so she might rock away
in front of the TV while old streets,
rooms and faces slowly fade.

And it's not even faith or certainty.
        No red earth, squawk of crows
        sunlight sharper than swords
        no clasping hand, chorus
        of familiar voices
        cicadas louder than the flight path
over crouching federation cottages.
        Just home. Or what we call it.
All my mementos: photos carefully placed
and posed. This is how I show myself –
        this cushion, this bathroom tile
        this brand of television screen.
My little nest I weave and toss and prune
and at the end, just things, just walls and
rooves and sparkly things that do not breathe.

My home lives in words
        in days undawned, blessed friends
        adored child, enduring man
        and mother of sighs.
All the rest is lies.

www.ingramcontent.com/pod-product-compliance
Lightning Source LLC
Chambersburg PA
CBHW050259120526
44590CB00016B/2416